W9-BWC-179

Date: 12/15/15

J 636.9332 MAT
Matzke, Ann H.,
Hedgehog /

PALM BEACH COUNTY
LIBRARY SYSTEM
3650 SUMMIT BLVD.
WEST PALM BEACH, FL 33406

HEDGEHOG

Ann Matzke

Rourke
Educational Media

rourkeeducationalmedia.com

Scan for Related Titles
and Teacher Resource

Before Reading:

Building Academic Vocabulary and Background Knowledge

Before reading a book, it is important to tap into what your child or students already know about the topic. This will help them develop their vocabulary, increase their reading comprehension, and make connections across the curriculum.

1. *Look at the cover of the book. What will this book be about?*
2. *What do you already know about the topic?*
3. *Let's study the Table of Contents. What will you learn about in the book's chapters?*
4. *What would you like to learn about this topic? Do you think you might learn about it from this book? Why or why not?*
5. *Use a reading journal to write about your knowledge of this topic. Record what you already know about the topic and what you hope to learn about the topic.*
6. *Read the book.*
7. *In your reading journal, record what you learned about the topic and your response to the book.*
8. *After reading the book complete the activities below.*

Content Area Vocabulary
Read the list. What do these words mean?

drawstring
frothy
high frequency
nocturnal
permit
predators
primitive
savannahs
snout
solitary
waddle

After Reading:

Comprehension and Extension Activity

After reading the book, work on the following questions with your child or students in order to check their level of reading comprehension and content mastery.

1. *Would a hedgehog make a great pet for your family? Explain. (Text to self connection)*
2. *How did the hedgehog get its name? (Summarize)*
3. *When may a hedgehog curl into a ball? (Asking questions)*
4. *Explain self-anointing. (Summarize)*
5. *How does the hedgehog's characteristics help it to survive? (Asking questions)*

Extension Activity

Hedgehogs are nocturnal animals. There are many other animals that are active at night. Think about animals that you hear around your house at night. What characteristics do those animals have that help it survive? How are they similar to the hedgehog?

Table of Contents

What Kind of Animal?

What animal gets its name from the shrubbery it searches for food and the pig-like grunting sound it makes? A hedgehog.

Hedgehogs are not your typical pet. These interesting and unusual **nocturnal** animals with bright eyes, sweet faces, and prickly backs require special care and handling.

Knowing more about hedgehogs will help you decide if it is the right pet for you.

Days of the Dinosaurs

Hedgehogs are one of the oldest, most **primitive** animals to roam the Earth since the time of dinosaurs.

Imagine these little animals sniffing and snuffling as they **waddle** along behind woolly mammoths or saber-toothed tigers. Not much has changed for the hedgehog since the days of its prehistoric relatives.

Hedgehogs are native to Europe, Asia, and Africa. The African Pygmy is the most common species kept as pets.

FUN FACT

There are 17 species of hedgehogs in the world. The most common pet species is the African Pygmy hedgehog. Other types kept as pets include the long-eared hedgehog and the Indian long-eared hedgehog.

Originally from Northern and Central Africa, they are at home in grasslands, **savannahs**, and scrub areas.

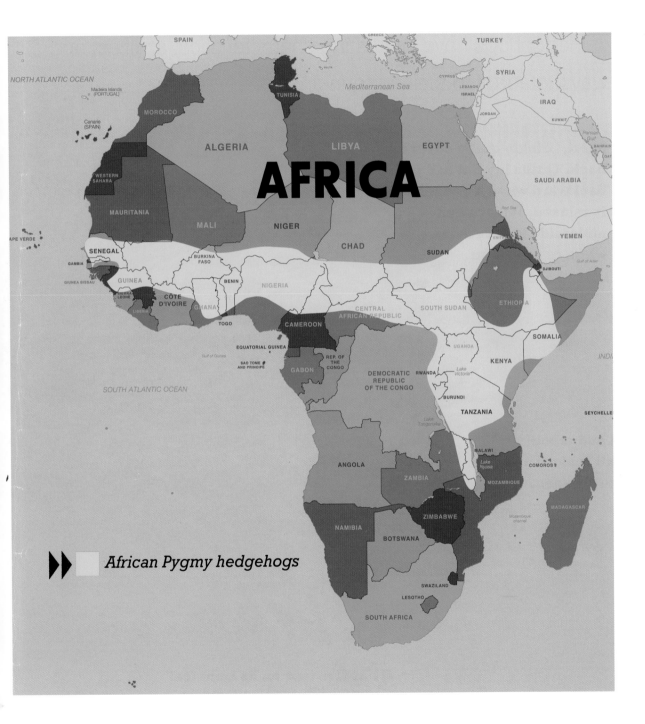

African Pygmy hedgehogs

From Head to Toe and Everything Between

Hedgehogs have interesting characteristics, abilities, and ways to adapt to their surroundings.

Short, prickly quills cover its back. Quills lay flat and point backward when a hedgehog is relaxed. Its face and underside is covered in soft white or brown fur. ⟩

A hedgehog's ⟩ tail is short and rarely seen.

⌒ It has five toes on its front feet and four toes on its hind feet. A hedgehog's rolling waddle comes from walking on the soles of its feet.

FUN FACT

Hedgehogs like to run and can travel up to a half mile during the night.

A hedgehog can hear the **high frequency** sounds of insects while listening for danger in the distance.

Longer whiskers help a hedgehog feel in the dark. Tiny, sensitive whiskers around the **snout** and mouth help it search for food.

A hedgehog has poor vision, even at night.

The hedgehog's senses of smell and taste are closely related. They help a hedgehog find food by smelling, licking, and tasting first. They can smell a worm one foot (.30 meters) underground.

11

Curling into a Ball

Muscles under the edge of a hedgehog's spiny coat control the position of the quills. A frightened hedgehog can roll into a ball, drawing the edges of its spiny coat together like a **drawstring**, with its head, belly, and feet tucked inside. The quills are not barbed or poisonous. They crisscross and offer protection from **predators** and falls. The quills also help it blend into its environment.

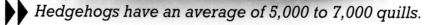

Hedgehogs have an average of 5,000 to 7,000 quills.

Quills

Quills are stiff hairs. They are thick, hollow on the inside, and lightweight. They are short, measuring from a quarter inch to one inch long (0.5 to 2.5 centimeters). Quills are smooth to touch but can be sharp on the ends.

Quills grow out of the skin and don't come loose. Adult hedgehog quills are permanent. Removal may injure the animal.

FUN FACT

Young hedgehogs lose the quills they are born with, replacing them with adult spines. This process is called quilling.

Is a Hedgehog the Right Pet?

Some states, counties, and districts do not allow hedgehogs as pets. Before buying one, check with local authorities. Even if it's legal to own a hedgehog you might need to buy a **permit**.

Local animal control agencies or your state's fish and wildlife department can help with permits.

Hedgehogs are not permitted in Arizona, California, Georgia, Hawaii, Pennsylvania, and Washington, DC.

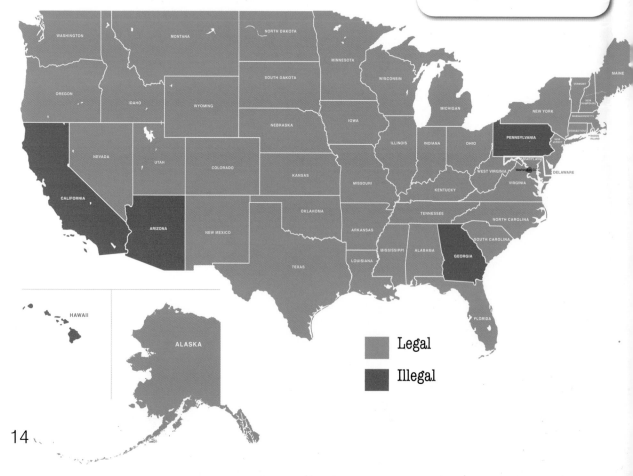

Legal

Illegal

What to Look for
When Selecting a Hedgehog

Don't be tempted to pick the first one you see. Try to choose from several hedgehogs. Spend time watching them because each has its own personality. Pick one up and wait for it to relax. They are friendly with people they trust. Look for one that is curious and bright-eyed with no visible drainage from its nose or ears.

FUN FACT

Hedgehogs can be litter trained like cats.

Home Sweet Home

Hedgehogs are **solitary** animals, which means they like to live alone. The scent of a dog or cat nearby can stress them out.

Pet Pointers

A pet hedgehog needs:

- an indoor rabbit cage or hutch without wire bottom
- a dark place to sleep and burrow, or a sleeping hut
- safe, easy to clean cage liner made from washable cloth or paper pellets
- heavy crock or bottle for water
- large exercise wheel
- heavy food bowl to prevent tipping
- plenty of places to hide
- a shallow litter box, open on one end and filled with pellet paper litter

African Pygmy hedgehogs come from a warm climate. They need the room temperature to be consistently between 75 and 80 degrees Fahrenheit (24 to 27 degrees Celsius).

A hedgehog's cage should be placed somewhere to receive 12 hours of daylight and 12 hours of darkness. They have sensitive ears so find a quiet, out of the way spot for the cage.

At night, when hedgehogs are awake, they are on the move. Don't let them get bored. A pet hedgehog needs plenty of toys, tubes, and hideaways to explore.

Welcome to the Family

Moving-in day can be stressful for hedgehogs. Keep noises down and speak softly. Introduce new things slowly.

Spend time getting to know one another. Friendly hedgehogs are handled often. Your hedgehog will soon recognize you by your scent.

Pet Pointers

You can help your hedgehog get to know your scent by wearing a T-shirt all day then draping it over your pet's cage.

 New lotions and perfumes can confuse your hedgehog because they cover up your original scent.

Handling a Hedgehog

Handle your hedgehog when it is awake. Be quiet and slow. Pick it up with your hands, not gloves. Put a hand on each side of your pet and slowly bring them together.

Set your new pet in your lap or another safe place in case it wiggles free. It may be shy at first. Be patient and gentle. Talk in a calm, quiet voice. Gently stroking it will help it relax. Reward your pet with a treat for good behavior.

Staying Fit and Healthy

Hedgehogs grow to be six to eight inches (15 to 20 centimeters) long and weigh 18 to 25 ounces (.51 to .70 kilograms). They live an average of five to eight years.

Hedgehogs need a balanced diet. Their daily intake should include:

- dry, hard food
- a few live insects as a treat
- a small amount of fresh fruits and vegetables

Consult a veterinarian about the specifics of your pet's diet.

▶▶ *Do not leave food out all day. Feed your hedgehog in the morning and evening when it is awake and most active.*

Finding a Veterinarian

It is important to find a veterinarian who is knowledgeable and cares for hedgehogs. Ask for recommendations when purchasing your hedgehog.

Keep the phone number handy for a 24-hour veterinary clinic in case of an emergency. If your hedgehog becomes ill or is injured, you want to seek medical help quickly.

Behavior

Hedgehogs are fast runners, good climbers, explorers, and escape artists. Make sure your pet's cage is safe and secure.

▶▶ *Hedgehogs like to hide in warm, dark places. To find a hiding hedgehog, get on your hands and knees and explore under and behind appliances and furniture.*

Grooming

Hedgehogs keep themselves fairly clean but occasionally you might need to give your pet a bath. In a small sink or basin, place your pet in about an inch of warm water. Using a spray bottle, spray warm water on the quills and gently clean the skin and quills with shampoo and a soft toothbrush. Rinse well, being careful to not get water or shampoo in its eyes, ears, nose, or mouth. Wrap your hedgehog in a smooth towel to dry. When the bath is over, reward your pet with a treat.

Bath Supplies
- spray bottle
- gentle hypo-allergenic shampoo
- soft toothbrush
- smooth towel

Self-Anointing

When hedgehogs smell or taste something strange, they can make a **frothy** saliva in their mouth. They'll spread the saliva across their quills with their long tongues. This is called self-anointing.

Sometimes it will be a couple of licks and other times they may spend several minutes covering their quills. Hedgehogs do this to smell like the new object. They also may cover themselves this way to cool down or protect themselves from something.

If the hedgehog doesn't clean off the dried saliva, you may need to give it a bath.

Fun Fact

Self-anointing is when an animal smears secretions or parts of other animals or plants on itself.

They may not be soft and cuddly like kittens or puppies, but hedgehogs are fascinating pets.

Things to Think About If You Want a Pet Hedgehog

- Can you have a hedgehog where you live?
- Can you provide the equipment needed?
- Do you have time to care for and interact with a hedgehog?
- Can you make the commitment for six to eight years?

Glossary

drawstring (DRAW-string): a string or cord that closes or tightens a bag or piece of clothing when you pull the ends

frothy (frawthee): lots of small bubbles in or on top of a liquid

high frequency (hye FREE-kwuhn-see): higher pitched sounds

nocturnal (nok-TUR-nuhl): to do with the night or happening at night

permit (pur-MIT): to allow something

predators (PRED-uh-turz): animals that hunt other animals for food

primitive (PRIM-uh-tiv): an early stage of development

savannahs (suh-VAN-uhs): flat grassy plains with few trees or no trees in tropical areas

snout (snout): the long, front part of an animal's head

solitary (SOL-uh-ter-ee): prefers to be alone

waddle (WAHD-uhl): to walk awkwardly, taking short steps and swaying from side to side

Index

Show What You Know

1. How long have hedgehogs been on Earth?

2. Which part of the world do hedgehogs come from?

3. Name two facts about hedgehogs' quills.

4. When are hedgehogs least active?

5. Name three things a hedgehog needs in their home.

Websites to Visit

www.coolkidfacts.com/hedgehog-facts-for-kids

www.kids.nationalgeographic.com/animals/hedgehog

www.hedgehogcentral.com/stats.shtml

About the Author

Ann H. Matzke is a children's librarian. She has an MFA in Writing for children and young adults from Hamline University. She grew up having many different kinds of pets: cats, fish, turtles, hamsters, gerbils and fire-bellied toads. Ann and her family live in Gothenburg, Nebraska with their chocolate lab, Penny and three cats, Max, Michael and Bean. Ann enjoys traveling, reading, and writing books for children.

Meet The Author!
www.meetREMauthors.com

© 2016 Rourke Educational Media

All rights reserved. No part of this book may be reproduced or utilized in any form or by any means, electronic or mechanical including photocopying, recording, or by any information storage and retrieval system without permission in writing from the publisher.

www.rourkeeducationalmedia.com

PHOTO CREDITS: Cover: ©Vvvvera; page 1: ©iravgustin; page 3: ©Kamonrat; page 4: ©lorenzo104; page5: ©Gertjan Hooijer; page 6-7: ©Corey Ford; page 6 (bottom): ©Lana Langlois; page 8, page 10-11: ©eve_eveolgenesis; page 12: ©aldra; page 13: ©Stephan Zabel; page 15: ©Dean Fika; page 16, page 17 (bottom), page 18 (top): ©Carmelka; page 17 (top): ©pagadesign; page 18 (bottom): ©gbh007; page 19: ©Cheungmily; page 20: ©Business Plus; page 21: ©Vasiliy Koval; page 22 (top): ©Pleprakaymas; page 22 (bottom), page 23, page 30: ©Best dog photo; page 24-26: ©SuperMeganAngle; page 27: ©Parushin; page 28: ©Eugene Kalenkovich; page 29: ©Oleg Kozlov

Edited by: Keli Sipperley

Cover design and Interior design by: Rhea Magaro

Library of Congress PCN Data

Hedgehog / Ann H. Matzke
(You Have a Pet What?!)
ISBN 978-1-63430-433-7 (hard cover)
ISBN 978-1-63430-533-4 (soft cover)
ISBN 978-1-63430-622-5 (e-Book)
Library of Congress Control Number: 2015931856

Also Available as:

ROURKE'S
e-Books

Printed in the United States of America, North Mankato, Minnesota